Letting Go

Also by Angela Topping

Solo Poetry Collections:
Dandelions for Mothers' Day (Stride 1988 and 1989)
The Fiddle: New and Selected Poems (Stride 1999)
The Way We Came (bluechrome 2007)
The New Generation (Salt 2010) for children
I Sing of Bricks chapbook (Salt 2011)
Catching On (Rack Press 2011)
The Lightfoot Letters (erbacce 2011)
Kids' Stuff (erbacce 2011) for children
Paper Patterns (Lapwing 2012)

Critical Works:
Focus on Spies by Michael Frayn (Greenwich Exchange 2008)
Focus on The Bloody Chamber and Other Stories by Angela Carter (Greenwich Exchange 2009)
Focus on Selected Poems by John Clare – Everyman Edition (Greenwich Exchange, forthcoming)

Editor:
The Least Thing (Stride 1989) Foreword by George Szirtes
Making Connections, A Festschrift for Matt Simpson (Stride 1996)
Sculpted: Poems of the North West, co-edited with Lindsey Holland (North West Poets 2013)

Co-author:
GCSE English Literature for OCR Student Book and Teacher Book (both OUP 2010)
OCR GCSE Poetry Anthology Student Book (OUP 2011)

Letting Go

Poems of childhood, daughterhood and parenthood

Mother's Milk Books

First published in Great Britain in 2013 by Mother's Milk Books

Introduction and cover design copyright © Teika Bellamy 2013
Front cover image 'Seeds' copyright © Lois Rowlands 2013

All poems copyright © Angela Topping
Copyright of the poetry resides with Angela Topping.

ISBN 978-0-9573858-1-8

Typeset in Georgia and Sheer Beauty by Teika Bellamy.
Printed and bound in Great Britain by The Russell Press, Nottingham,
on FSC paper and board sourced from sustainable forests.
www.russellpress.com

First published in 2013 by Mother's Milk Books
www.mothersmilkbooks.com

For Dave, Laura and Rosie

How selfhood begins with a walking away,
And love is proved in the letting go.

C. Day Lewis

ACKNOWLEDGEMENTS

Some of these poems are taken from previous collections:

These poems appeared in *Dandelions for Mothers' Day* (Stride 1988): 'Sitting with Dad', 'Two for Dad', 'Cleaning the Brasses', 'Dandelions for Mothers' Day', 'Last Gifts', 'Visiting Granddad', 'Twll Din, Mr Lloyd', 'Ultrasound', 'Until Morning', 'A Casting Off'. From *The Fiddle* (Stride 1999): 'Dirt', 'She Leaves her Body to Science', 'Broken Tokens', 'Tending the Plot', 'Granny Coyne', 'Equal Measures', 'Final Examination', 'House of Cards', 'Just a Minute', 'Prospect from a Bay', 'From the Wendy House', 'Mothers Shopping', 'Photograph Day', 'Father's Bronchitis', 'Father, Gardening', 'First Five Metres', 'The Mother', 'Passing it On', 'Things She Lost'. From *The Way We Came* (bluechrome 2007): 'Second Best', 'Seconds Out on Saturdays', 'Players Navy Cut', 'The Attic'. From *The New Generation* (Salt 2010): 'Kenning My Dad', 'Friends', 'My Best Friend'. From *Kids' Stuff* (erbacce 2011): 'Kids' Stuff'. From *I Sing of Bricks* (Salt 2011): 'Bildungsroman', 'Kitchen Ghosts', 'Words of Love'. From *The Lightfoot Letters* (erbacce 2011): 'Ada'. From *Paper Patterns* (Lapwing 2012): 'Paper Patterns', 'Monochrome', 'Salve'. 'Dr Love' was commissioned for *Split Screen*, edited by Andrew Jackson (Red Squirrel 2011); First published in *Musings on Mothering* edited by Teika Bellamy (Mother's Milk Books 2012): 'Letting Go'.

Appearing in print for the first time: 'Little Dishwasher', 'Reverse Routes', 'In the Interval', 'Silver Chains', 'Moving Out', 'Laura's Room', 'A Posy for our Daughter on her Wedding Day'.

CONTENTS

Her knitting bag was needle-sharp and full —
unfinished work and ball and ball of wool.

What should I do with broken tokens now?

He knows the names
of all wild things
in the earth and sky.

They want me for Mother, darning socks, sewing pockets,
worrying what to cook them for their tea.

She swam in a booming cave,
fathoms down.

But they learn to walk away
like any other guest.

*

INTRODUCTION

by Teika Bellamy, Editor, Mother's Milk Books

In autumn 2011, when I put a call out for submissions for the fundraising anthology, *Musings on Mothering*, I was inundated with work. One of the poets who contacted me was Angela Topping. The poems she submitted touched me deeply with their sincerity and humanity. These were poems crafted with much love and skill.

I wanted to include all the poems that Angela had sent me, but the anthology was already bursting at the seams, so I published the ones that sat comfortably within some of the major themes of the book.

We kept in touch after the book was published. I found out more about her previous publications and, as finances allowed, bought her poetry collections. When I received each book I felt a thrill of excitement — here were more wonderful poems to read, *feel* and savour.

Some of the collections were — outrageously! — out of print. An idea began to form in my mind. What if *I* could publish some of Angela's work? I suggested as much to her, and was delighted to discover that she didn't think my idea was completely ridiculous! We back-and-forthed; she thought a themed collection could work well, including poems about mothers, fathers, children — as well as breastfeeding, of course.

She worked on the manuscript, and one day it arrived in my email inbox. That evening, when my children were fast asleep — all household chores completed — I allowed myself the pleasure of reading it. During the reading I found myself in tears. And then I was laughing, and then smiling. When I came to the end of the manuscript, I knew I had to publish it.

So here it is; Angela's manuscript made real, into paper and ink (or pixels!) along with Lois Rowlands's stunning photography on the cover. I hope that like me, you will read *Letting Go* and *feel* its quietly passionate lyricism.

*

From Sheila Kitzinger, social anthropologist of birth, birth educator and writer

'A lovely rainbow of poems to have at your side as you greet new life and breastfeed your baby, and whenever you want to think about those to whom you have said goodbye.'

Angora is soft and loves you...

Sitting with Dad

I loll on the safe floor
between my father's feet,
and he is arms, back,
deep cushions. I pick
at dainties from his plate.
His words rock me.

If outsiders come to call,
I scale his chair's heights,
scramble into his space
as he sits perching forward.
I curl up snug behind
the shelter of his back,
snuff the warm scent of him.

Now my place is cold and vast.
I fidget in chairs, lack a favourite,
learn discomfort, stand alone.

Two for Dad

Blackberry...

In it together:
conspiring against bramble,
holding down a spray
of beauties for me to pick,
showing how leaves
hide choicest fruit.

Finding docks to cool
nettled flesh, stained,
battlescarred, spoils dangling
in baskets, on handlebars,
we ride our triumph home.

...Pies

We dare not go through the kitchen
when you bake. There is
deftness, artistry at work.

The pies are crammed
with blackberries, plump
with pleasure at being picked.
A line of flour on your jumper
from rolling out.

The pinched edges of pastry
seal the boozy juice.
You cut large slices
to offer me.

Cleaning The Brasses

You'd bring out Brasso, rags,
spread newspapers: Dad to apply,
us to polish. Candlesticks,
copper kettle, easy teapot,
bells, bowls, great plaques that rang
when struck by a working rag:
years of such afternoons white
between the picture's embossed lines and curves.
Rank in our nostrils the stink of metal polish
and black transferring from brass to hands.

These adorners of your fireplaces
claimed by relatives. I remember
the day you gave up polishing,
wrapped them in newspaper, begging us
to have them. We had other plans.
No time to spend afternoons
changing tarnish into burnish.

Why then did I take candlesticks,
two pairs, one tall, one squat?
To show me again you sitting back on heels
admiring brass beaded with light
glint in the darkening room.

Dandelions for Mothers' Day

"Pee-the-Beds" and "Mother-Die!"
"Pick it and your mam'll die!"

"Faces like the sun," she said,
plunged them in a jam-jar.

But they caught up with her:
stained her skin yellow,
turned her hair to seed-clocks,
blew away her years.

Bildungsroman

I

Angora is soft and loves you
smothers you and makes you itch;
its fluffy aura glows like a candle flame.
Mother says, "Keep it on; it's cold out."

I'm sitting in my pram, bound up
in leather reins, chin-tied bonnet,
knitted mittens. The pram's apron
is fastened, the hood is a canvas tent.
I'm waiting.

II

Mother's handbag, faintly musty,
old and blackly polished. Inside
a half-used lipstick, old receipts,
crushed handkerchiefs she'd scrabble for
to dab my face, a spit and polish wash
on the bumpy homeward groaning of the bus.

She'd never keep letters or photos
in her bag, since the day
she'd lost one with all my father's
love letters. They could take her worn purse,
its few pound notes, stamps, copper and silver,
but not her private hoarded memories.

III

I'd never dare to rummage through
her closely guarded privacy, or pry
in drawers crammed with lace, though I'd
try her wedding dress for size, browse
her jewellery in its purple velvet box:
paste brooches and clip-on earrings.
I'd swivel this way and that to catch
Hollywood nymphet poses,
sideways eyes coy and flirty.

IV

She wanted to wrap me up, keep me young,
but I chafed against restraints,
wanted to answer for myself, learn Latin,
crack codes. I ran around the corner;
the school bus yanked me miles away.

Monochrome

A candid photograph, a moment caught
in black and white, nineteen fifty nine,
a council house estate interior.
A television, first they ever saw,
holds two small girls in rapture where they lie,
on bellies, heads propped up by hands, enthralled,
unaware that they were captured too
in spying camera's eye. Behind them
father monitors, one eye on them
the other focused on the flickering screen.
He has arranged for this new-fangled thing
and feels some pride in its unveiling day.
He never lived to see its colours show.
His camera was only monochrome.
But in this photograph, the magic gadgets
are cutting-edge, brand new, and he
is master of the revels, bestowing love.

Seconds Out on Saturdays

Saturday afternoons:
the alien atmosphere
of wrestling on the telly.

No speech or mithering.
Just watch as one fat man
slams another down.

A pugilistic referee shouts
Seconds out. Worse
than playground fights.

Grown men, slathered with
sweat, grunt while my father,
brothers, egg them on.

And Mother in the kitchen,
presiding over suds,
wrestles with sheets.

Equal Measures

My father cutting Cheshire
gauged by eye the placing of the wire,
shaved from crumbling block
the perfect ounce.

This skill he had to live by,
dividing creamy cartwheels
under Mr Lennon's
judging eye.

His father's careless cheeseparing
cheated him of grammar school.
His childhood left
a bitter taste.

Not wanting us to gag on rind,
he jiggled scales to weigh
in equal measure
everything,

his knife scrupulous. But we
just kids, repaid him with
"Got more than me!"
"Got more than me!"

Father, you should not have left
until I'd told you what you meant.

Paper Patterns

Make me a dress the colour of sky
just after a June sunset, or one
like that velvet in George Henry Lee's
expensive Christmas window.

God love her, she'd try. Her mouth
prickled with a metal smile of pins
as she unrolled market-stall cloth,
spread crackling paper patterns.

She'd labour on at her Singer,
her small feet dancing the two-step
on the treadle, tunelessly humming,
secure in motherly skills.

But I failed to measure up, came to
dread her home-sewn lumpy seams,
gave up romance, took to wearing
lumberjack shirts, cut-down jeans.

Doctor Love

Jon Pertwee as The Third Doctor

Doctor, Doctor, when you first called I was nine.
I couldn't come with you then, still hiding behind daddy,
sheltering in his shadow in front of our monochrome set
dreaming of Gallifrey, of diving into your kaleidoscope.

I was changing like you, renewing all my cells,
going through to my third incarnation:
a new version of myself with pointed breasts, long hair,
a waist. Not nylon slacks but Levi's, lace and scent.

Doctor, Doctor, oh you dandy, velvet smoking jacket,
bow ties and leather gloves, you lounge lizard.
My mother warned me about men like you.
And yet you were the perfect gentleman, like daddy.

I watched as you outfaced Silurians, always polite
but not afraid to punch when words failed,
reverse the polarity and get the hell out of there.
I was getting out too: boys, A levels, university.

Doctor, Doctor, your world was colour like mine.
We watched you in black and white but knowing
others could see your green, burgundy and blue
as you strutted in galaxies, finding yourself, like me.

Daddy's girl learned to argue, teenstruck and difficult.
I had no TARDIS to travel back to myself. You
could have made everything alright again.
Where were you? Too busy on missions to call again.

Doctor, Doctor, you missed your chance with me.

25

Father's Bronchitis

I listen for
the creak of panic in his lungs
as he leans on pedals to confront
a hill.

I know his days on bikes are slowing,
the cycle chain ticks off the miles.
Trees and fields and lanes slip by.
And years.

I clutch my sheaf of flowers tight
knowing the house will stifle them.
He sits by open kitchen door,
for air,

gasping like a landed carp.
There's nothing I can do except
brew up the way he likes, put away
the bike.

Players Navy Cut

My father, asthmatic, always smoked.
At seventeen he was sophisticate, biting on a pipe,
impressing my gauche mother with his film-star looks.

Players Navy Cut was the brand of fags he liked.
I loved the cherry smell that clung
to folded silver paper begged from the boxes

but hated the stains made by a lit cigarette
burning on the side of the bath while he spent
hours locked in there reading the paper.

Hated his smoking, as mother had grown to,
once we realised he was killing himself slowly.
He liked saving up his vouchers; it seemed

the more he smoked, the more he could
write away for, in his well-tutored copperplate.
The picture of a salty sailor on the packet,

head wreathed by tarry rope, had come to be
my father as he might have been if his father
had let him join the navy at eighteen.

Smoking was his way of being carefree,
the sailor he might have become,
white-bearded, weathered, venerable.

Father, Gardening

He is nowhere now
so I can place him here,
leaning on a rake
plotting colour schemes,
knowing our garden's best.

He moves into the greenhouse
to cup the warm weight
of tomatoes in his hand.
Each plant is knotted,
rigged with twine and cane
in terracotta pot, like a galleon
earthed in its bottle.

There's nowt like Ailsa Craig,
he'd say, whispered name
mingling with green incense,
the intimate spice of tomatoes
and my father telling secrets.

Better there than in the ruined garden,
his greenhouse shattered and glassless.
Mowing lawns left him *out of puff,*
defeated. He'd stare through the window
at stacked terracotta pots,
some cracked with frost, watching —
in rain he dare not go out in —
red peonies smash to the ground.

Words of Love

I tried to tell you
but words came slow
for once, at least.
Such things are not easy.

Father, you left us
before I could say
what you'd always meant
despite the years we fought.

I was daddy's girl.
The day I was born
you walked into work
ten feet tall, mother said.

You, 44 years old
ready to love a dandling
last chance child,
teach her your ways.

You slept with a photo of me
nine years old and ringletted,
the image of my mother,
framed by your bed.

That last evening
I wanted to tell you
but you were not a man
to talk to of such things.

I sat an hour with you.
Wished you a better sleep
than last night's troubled one.
But you never woke again.

An hour later, the call came.
Mother found you, still warm.
Father, you should not have left
until I'd told you what you meant.

·

Final Examination

i.m. my father 1911-1978

Finals: the shining room,
measuring rows of desks.
Among pens and rulers, polo mints,
my sprig of rosemary curled.
Ancient Greeks would thread it
in their hair to sharpen wits.
I bruised the sword-shaped leaves,
began to write.

Now, in a hushed and darkened room,
you're tricked out in your best;
a box lined with satin — the blue
of rosemary in bloom. The herb
Remembrance is squeezed to cast
into your coffin, its green tongues
to writhe and shrivel in your flame.

As if I could forget... who wait
for the boom of your voice, the weight
of your tread, who quicken always
at some flat-capped grey head,
broad back, deliberate pace
still going somewhere, testing me,
holding all the answers now.

Reverse Routes

The car takes us the short way
from home to church, Dad
enduring his false teeth, me
in unfamiliar clothes: white
dress and veil, clutching his arm.
He is keeping me safe.
My lips are clamped, white freesias
trembling in my hand. Minutes before
I'd seen myself in mum's cheval mirror.
He'd told me he felt proud.

Not a man to talk to of feelings:
He'd never been able to hear
me cry, or bear my tear-stained cheeks.

The car glides past the roundabout,
The Crow's Nest pub, the corner shop
where we'd buy Sunday papers,
chocolate for me, in the life I was leaving.
It moves past the pavement where
I'd roller-skated with my friends.
Now I am a woman, twenty-one,
and the groom is waiting. After
the photo, we begin the long slow
walk up the aisle to my future.
Dad's steps are steady as heartbeats.
He loves me enough to let me go.

Two years later, months into a hollow winter
and it is I who must let my father go.

Dad is lying down ahead of us,
swathed in white flowers, as we make
the reverse journey from church.
The funeral car pauses outside our house,
where I no longer live. Mum clutches my arm.

Her knitting bag was needle-sharp, and full —

unfinished work, and ball on ball of wool.

Second Best

She'd never wanted to outlive his care,
his dogged strength, his cups of tea at nine,
gas fire and telly on, his firm hand holding hers.
She wept within my arms, light as a child.
I never thought he'd let me down like this
while upstairs elder brother knelt beside
the bed where our dead father lay. Less than
an hour before, I'd wished my dad good night,
a better sleep than his last, troubled one.

Two years later, straight from work, I ran
to join the ward's impatient queue.
Your dad was first in every night, she said.

She Leaves her Body to Science

I am giving up.
No-one could desire this body.
Never had much hair
down there, underneath,
and even that thin silk has gone.
Unbuttoned from flowered cotton
breasts that fed four babies —
no use to anyone now.

Years ago I had to refuse a doctor.
He wanted all his students to watch
THAT examination. "I'd rather die,"
I'd said, for hadn't mother taught me
"Nice girls keep their knees together"?

No-one's ever seen me get undressed.
What happened in the dark
was love and wanting babies.
He was so handsome, your father.
I gave birth in a decorous manner,
ladylike, just mother and a midwife.
Cleansed afterwards in church
with Holy Water, Candles, Prayers.

I signed forms today.
Those doctors who whisper at my bed's end
desire me. I am interesting to them.
They want to probe my belly,
name organs, count my ribs.

Last Gifts

I have to undo railings to get close,
coax her to take water. My mother
in a cot, sipping a baby's cup.

Face almost hers under the fretted hair.
On hospital bed familiar hands falter.
She has too much to say, and words are rags.

She scans an inch of vision till she finds
my face. My hand between hers, she urges
"I love you very much".

Eyes swim beyond the waiting room,
no longer knowing me, ears deaf to my goodbyes.
Only the struggle to breathe, the waiting.

*

Secretly, a girlchild begins
unfolding into grief.

A Casting-Off

She sits and briskly knits, her needles clack,
and grimly add the seconds of her life.
Her head is bent so she won't see his chair
whose vacancy insists "no longer wife."

She chooses factory-wound wool, as skeins
would underline his absence, sharpen need
for deft controlling thumbs to gather threads,
his held-out arms that always took the lead.

And at her knee she taught me purl and plain;
she'd pick up stitches, undo and put right
my every tangle; tackle garter, rib,
till lymph, and blood, and bile snapped off her light.

Her knitting bag was needle-sharp, and full —
unfinished work, and ball on ball of wool.

What should I do with broken tokens now?

Broken Tokens

In their padded, bought-in box I keep
what still remains of diamonds and of gold.
Too good to last, too pure to wear, the rings
he bought her first, now sliver thin and old.

What should I do with broken tokens now?
He hasn't gone to sea, and she can't wait
his safe return on shore. And this cooled gold
is trinket that can never be remade.

Prospect from a Bay
(Halton View, Widnes)

I've stood in that bay window in my parents' room
countless times: soft-soaping whining toddlers
radaring for returning mums and dads —
my brothers and sisters chasing time —
or scanning for careless boyfriends
until dad's clock whispered unwelcome truths.
Many's the time I've swung my legs
from the blanket-box seat, humouring him
as, ill in bed, he sipped the tea I'd brought.

You could see the field across the road,
the factory where even dad was overshadowed
by powerhouse engines. Sunsets bloodied the sky
over my *Bongs* territory, its secret paths
patiently mapped, its countries and geography
named by adventurer me: *The Chalk Downs,
The Plateau, Rainbow River* — dyed by chemicals.
The Chemics industry stained our family's lives,
blistered our paintwork, hastened deaths.

Others look through that window now,
viewing sunsets and the long dry road.
The *Bongs* is just wasteground.

Tending the Plot

Of all human activities, apart from the procreation of children,
gardening is the most optimistic and hopeful.

Susan Hill

On her knees she toiled
the narrow allotment of sour soil
shovelled above her parents' coffins.
Her fingers teased out roots.

I was sent to fetch water,
to rinse green scum from the jar
where flowers were left to die.

Now she's buried there herself,
husband's ashes at her halted feet.
The plot's full and snug as families,
the black stone chock-a-block with facts.

I'm bent-backed elsewhere,
uprooting weeds, fumbling seed,
coaxing from the damp earth
all the colour and the scent I can.

House of Cards

In those wardrobes no-one wants
mother hung her Sunday best;
on those shelves father's sweaters
were stacked beside coiled leather belts.
From this hook braces jangled.

In the loft squat plastic bags
of blobby paintings, hand-made cards,
with rounded script declaring love.
No time now to clear them out.
Best leave them sealed, like scars.

Behind new wallpaper lie surfaces
once brushed against, a diary of pattern.
New owners will scrape away
our strata, brick up doorways,
suiting our house to their needs.

Miles away in other towns
we brace ourselves to feel the house of cards
huffed down.

Just a Minute
(Radio 4)

Today my kids are skipping
over your threshold and you not here.
The ones you never dandled,
pronounced prodigies: My kids
who only know your photograph.

I'm busy clearing the path
that twenty years ago I skipped
to find you at kitchen table,
sweating in a vest, wheezing,
door open for the draught.

Your eyes follow me as I go back
and forth with dolls, drinks, books
to make an island paradise on the lawn.
Your face is weatherbeaten brown,
white upper arms are soft baby flesh.

As you sip black tea, your bitter cup,
you listen to the radio.
It's *Just a Minute*, just a minute ago.

Kitchen Ghosts

Steps echo on terracotta tiles
but no-one's there.

In the morning
someone's washed the pots,
left them gleaming
piled high
in a white china mountain.
The drainer's neat,
a small cloth wrung out,
draped over the tap.
Crumbs have been
brushed up. On scrubbed table
one empty tea mug stands.
Father's mug. Always
drank his tea black.
That's how I know.

I can see his workaday hands
never tiring of setting things straight.

He is expecting Mother,
wonders when she'll come.
Each morning, I hope for
lemon drizzle cake, two
pieces missing,
two empty cups.

He knows the names
of all wild things
in the earth and sky.

Granny Coyne

My granny's a whispering woman,
her stories follow me down the hall;
hang, half-told, in the corners of the kitchen
above a tut-tut of metal knitting pins.

My granny's a soothing woman,
smoother of brows with a cool palm;
polisher of brasses; igniter of fires;
she picks up babies before they cry.

My granny's a loving woman,
shoes clucking on tiles when I call.
Her eyes laugh at me in photographs.
She'd have loved you, my mother says.

Little Dishwasher

i.m. Peter Coyne

You wanted a houseful of children,
sons. When your only child, a daughter
made a polite appearance, you said
a little dishwasher. You didn't mean
any disrespect; a boy would have
carried the family name, been a modest
pride for you. Through two world wars —
you serious in your uniform, did
the thought of her sustain you?

And when you lay dying, cancer
robbing you of all your fight,
you said to her as she washed you
how glad I am of my little dishwasher.
She who could shape a story
gave me this memory, a gift passed down
like a brassoed medal, to me,
your granddaughter, the one you never met.

Ada
(1882-1933)

How I begin to know you through these letters.
In 1923 she was away from home, your girlie,
leaving behind three clumsy boys
and two baby daughters to plague you.

That winter was so harsh
the wind blew the pictures off the wall
and your cough gusted through the house,
your chest creaked like old floorboards
and you wrote of everything you did,
saving scraps of gossip about secret weddings
to piece together with the oppression
of household chores, the perils
of ironing with a badly-cut thumb,
the days it took the washing to dry
and little Dorothy going *worse naughty*,
smashing all the plates, while namesake Ada
screamed and yowled because she did not know
like older ones, how to write a letter.

The house must have quietened at night
while the boys laboured over their letters;
my father's carefully neat, Vincent's scrawled,
not yet master of his pen, and you're exhausted
but no power can stop you writing page after page
in your carefully flowing script. For doesn't
a mother cat cry when a kitty is lost.
Ada, grandmother, how alike we are
two mothers looking out for our dear ones.

Visiting Granddad

I

The bike is leaned against a wall,
I'm lifted down, a gate unlatched;

Led up the yard he used to play in,
weeks of tea leaves in the drain;

Through fusty kitchen to a room
whose fire glares, rising in its grate.

My outdoor things keep me safe
from their strangers' claim on me.

A clock shouts from the mantel, filling words
that father, son, stepmother reach to use.

He holds out his arms. I edge
closer to dad, try "Going now?".

II

I've never been upstairs before.
I've never come in at the front
or been brought by mum and yet
our visit has been pre-arranged.

The tall man who is grandfather
and of whom I am afraid

is lying in a high brass bed
while women fuss and mother stands

diminished. Like a glinting skull
below his bed a chamber pot
appals. All I can think about
is what might lurk within.

I'm held up to kiss his warm
and briny cheek, to say good bye
to a man I've never really known
or touched before today.

My daddy's dad, though something's wrong
I'm never told. He must have asked
for me, the littlest one. My kiss
brought him back to life again.

My Best Friend

We stand on the riverbank
while he shows me
where trout lie.

He knows the names
of all wild things
in the earth and sky.

He taught me colours
and animal prints,
bought me a kite.

We laugh a lot.
He tells old jokes
to make things right.

We play cards for money —
old pennies he's saved.
He's my best mate.

He buys me chips
in a drippy vinegar bag.
My grandad's great.

Friends

He was a tall black Arab,
she was five years old,
the first black person
she had ever seen.

It was love at first sight.

He was big and gentle,
sat her on his knee,
called her a little lady,
taught her strange new facts.

His list of continents began with Africa.

They were always together.
In his home he was a teacher.
She loved his beautiful skin,
his soft curly hair.

Now she knew the world differently.

Walking in the garden
she only reached his knee,
her small hand resting
in his huge strong fist.

Only later did she know
how her father had
defended him from
people in the street.

How could anyone not love
Nasr Hassan Abbas?
His very name was a poem.
A shelter from any storm.

Now she knew the world differently.

They want me for Mother, darning socks, sewing pockets, worrying what to cook them for their tea.

From The Wendy House

Peter Pan: The Opera House, Manchester

"Cramful of adventures" he'd promised, but this place
is packed with scruffy boys who can't stop
walking planks and smoking peace pipes —
games they think too rough for me, their Wendy-bird.
They want me for Mother, darning socks, sewing pockets,
worrying what to cook them for their tea.

Peter doesn't really want to hear of Cinderella's bliss,
would have her picking over lentils,
peeling spuds forever, never find her Prince.
It wouldn't be so bad if he'd play with me
but he wants to be one of the boys, not prepared
for Fatherhood. Why is it me that must grow up?

Yanking me from a warm nursery for this!
Whizzing my head with dazzling words, making me
feel light enough to soar between the stars.

Mothers Shopping

These older mothers have no strollers
to heave uphill loaded with shopping.
They have borne their children years before
and now are shopping for them, bearing home
one bulging bag in each hand, balancing.

Wide hips and huge bums sway from side
to side as their veined legs, sore feet
carry them painfully rolling in boat shoes.
Breasts an extra burden in their big coats.

Somewhere at home, dusty under beds,
are biscuit tins of sepia photographs —
themselves in three-ply jumpers, cultured pearls,
hair coiffured as now in too-tight curls,
their skin a soft bloom. You can trace
the ghosts of their delicate cheekbones.

Twll Din, Mr Lloyd

Bristling with nurse's authority —
"Me that knows" and "They drummed it into us" —
she dismisses "all those books", hands down
policies of clout-casting, buys warm vests.

She's given up fingering my sills and mantels,
pities my lack of scouring skills, admits
I iron well, knows her son is happy, amply fed.
Her bandages herringbone our wounds.

She trades teasings with us, offers impudences,
screws up her face to do silly voices.
Tells how Ewart shook warm wee-wee drops
into Megan's posh moisturiser jar:
their two heads round doors baiting her smugness,
"Pee cream, pee cream, good for the complexion!"
Once she took a friend home, polite in tutored Welsh,
to good-evening her father with "Arse Hole, Mr Lloyd".

Photograph Day

A knot of mothers is drawn tight.
Children fray nerves, unravel them.
They wait for the canvas pavilion,
a camera on a tripod, the giddy photographer.

Captured on film is a moment
where no party is progressing
and the pintucked child is smiling
from no particular happiness;
a professional smile for no-one
but the photographer.

The Mother

This child whose heart beats with mine
who shares my blood
is not for me.

The drumbeat of his heels
will not pound to my rhythms for long.

The milk tingling my breasts
will not be his food forever, and my hands
cannot be filled with his downed head.

From the moment the ovum
began its revolutions,
the moment he began to squirm
he was not mine.

When the cervix opens, spent tulip,
when pain clutches
when his head is ringed with fire
I must learn unloving.

Until his body slithers free
until his heels are clear
until he's lifted into arms

he's mine.

She swam in a booming cave,

fathoms down.

Ultrasound

We were spies on her world —
her safe house of skin. She
was etched in silver: moving, human.

She swam in a booming cave,
fathoms down. Heavy rope mooring her.
Round face, round eyes, ooh of mouth.

Gingerbread baby, currant eyes.
At home, I twist wool around needles,
craft garments, every stitch a wish.

Until Morning

Her cry bubbles. In a drowse,
I reach for her, fumbling bedclothes,
and settle her weight in my arm's crook,
unbuttoning.

Searching with tongue, eager, she fastens
mouth on nipple, fingers dimpling my skin.
Eyelashes on cheeks, she sucks us both asleep.

In the Interval

I dreamt I put her to the breast again,
lifting the right globe of milky weight,
baring a taut nipple for her eager mouth
in the front row stall of the red plush theatre.

It must have been the interval. Nothing
was happening onstage, and nearby
people queued for ice-cream, or slipped to the bar.
My baby doesn't have to go that far.

We become a diversion, people stop to chat.
"Is she enjoying herself?" "Isn't she clever
to wait till the interval for her milkshake?"
Not a single person seems to mind

one small baby quietly sucking a breast,
her pudgy hands entwining the bra strap,
my glorious breast tingling with satisfaction.
In a dream nothing is astonishing.

Kenning My Dad

He comes home smelling of outside
a bootstamping coat remover.
When he sits at the table
he's a food exterminator
a coffee-consuming pudding praiser.
He's a mountain strider, birdwatcher,
a cheering on at rugby shouter
a dolls' house maker, breadbaker,
cooking pasta in the kitchen on Sunday.
He's a vegetable nurturer
digging in the garden in the rain
a leekbringer, soup inventor.
at work he's a computer tapper
brainworker, travelling on a train worker.
At home he's our dad —
a bighugging loudlaughing funloving
daft teasing dad with a prickly face.

The First Five Metres

Wanting too much, I feared
the spat of blood, counted
weeks to twenty-eight.

A long journey, and now
she's washed up in my arms,
small survivor, snuggled in wool.

Her eyes question everything:
the ticking nurses,
the new father's beard.

She tongues the nipple,
half-interested, while her eyes
study the window's blank rectangle.

Cut loose from babyhood,
seven years of questions
fizz her eyes today,

launching herself into water
without arm-bands for the first time,
swimming, swimming away.

Kids' Stuff

Hanging round parks for a go on the swings
palms smelling of metal on the roundabout.
The iron grip of the slide as you launch yourself —
It's kids' stuff but I still like it.

Dipping your fingers in sherbet and licking
sticking your tongue down into ice cream
strengthening your suck on a thick milk shake —
It's kids' stuff but I still like it.

Playing follow-my-leader when no one can see
tidying your dolls' house and making them speak
cuddling your teddy when you can't get to sleep —
It's kids' stuff but I still like it.

Reading Narnia books and travelling with hobbits
watching E. Nesbit's books on TV
curling up in a chair with a book and some chocolate —
It's kids' stuff but I still like it.

Making shapes with bread dough and watching them rise
making gingerbread men with currants for eyes
putting smarties on top of little iced cakes —
It's kids' stuff but I still like it.

Going to the pictures to watch Walt Disney
getting sticky fingers from toffeed popcorn
sucking an ice-lolly through the second half —
It's kids' stuff but I still like it.

People try and tell you, you ought to grow up
my kids don't mind having a daft mum.
I don't see why I should stop having fun —
It's kids' stuff but I still like it.

Things She Lost

Mother gave the dolls' house
to neighbours' children. She had
so much, they so little. All the same
it shocked her, seeing it there.
Mother might've asked.

She lost her hamster. One night
it squeezed between the bars
of its home and vanished.
A taste for freedom given it
by too much play.

She lost her friend, kissing him.
He became Boyfriend.
Two years later he left her
for a younger woman.
It wouldn't have worked.

Next thing to go was virginity.
She didn't miss it, wondered why
she'd bothered holding on so long,
fear, probably, or the monster, trust.

Her figure went missing,
holding in the world;
flat stomach turned to globe.
First one child, then another.
Lost herself in motherhood.

Miniature lips open to bite

her breast and answer back.
Hands cling to hers, then
one day want their freedom.

One by one old selves
were rinsed away with the mornings,
lines on her face. Long ago
she lost her parents, watching them
become strangers, knowing death.

She let her grasp slip
from smaller things — that china
biscuit barrel with pie-frilled lid;
scrapbook of citrus wrappers
handed in at junior school
lost in some stockroom.

So many collections dispersed
in a life less than forty years.
So many days not worth remembering;
so many friends without addresses;
so many pretty birds flown.

Passing It On

I weigh out exact divisions
of flour and fat, mix with milk
as grandma, sixty years dead, used to do.
You both insist on dragging chairs
to stand halting each elbow
as I roll out onto floured board.

You lean to swipe strips of dough
pestering with questions while I
pinch and trim and tailor
pastry to plates. Parallel lines
slit the centre to let out steam.
With flourish of knife and brush
I cut and glue veined leaves of dough.

For loss of swiftness I've traded
continuity. 'My mother did it this way'
you'll both say to hampering audiences
as you mix with milk and deftly press your knives.

Dirt

The children flinch from the dead goldfish.
With averted eyes, we bury it at sea,
flushed down the toilet.
Things dead become dirty.

Death spreads like fungus.
Walking carefully in churchyards is taught
like table manners, simple courtesy.
Stepping on a grave is touching
at two removes, death's dirt.

My father, dead, was far from dirt.
Posh with his teeth in, best suit on,
all dressed up and nowhere to go,
yet I feared to touch him.

Step away. Stretch the sheet across
so we do not have to see
what we cannot understand.
Speak in whispers so as not
to soil our living tongues.

But they learn to walk away

like any other guest.

The Attic

To enter the attic is to be lost.
Up the ladder into the too warm
fly-trapping darkness beneath the eaves
to find an old dressing up frock
or Christmas presents carefully hidden
over the sleeping heads of the children.

Boxes full of secrets and memories,
things we can't bear to discard.
Open a box and baby cardigans
stained from mixed feeding
appeal to be used again. Old letters
unfold themselves in remembering hands.

Silver Chains

The stripes are silvered on my skin,
not for common view; my secret signs,
whispering I love you in tracery,
scripted onto my belly and thighs;
intricate as silver chains, glistening tracks
of snails on morning rugs, when they have
crept into the house, tasting the night silences.
Insignia of motherhood, cuneiform,
canticles of breathing space, mother-marks,
I will wear them all my life.

Adolescent

Suddenly girl-shaped at twelve,
showing a waist and little hips,
proud on her chest the first swellings
of breasts. Hungers have begun.

Like Janus, she is: one face turned
towards dolls, dolls' house a daily joy;
one face to womankind, wearing lace,
learning the mirror arts.

Moving Out

I was your mother
not much older
than you are now.

You were my dream
made flesh, my daughter.
So much more real

than I could ever
have imagined, from your
electric cries, your smiles

your running, climbing steps,
your insistent speech,
your fierce love.

For you I relinquished
looks I didn't know I had,
my girlhood, freedom.

And look at you now.
Beautiful, brave, strong
as you ever were.

Far from my arms
but never gone.
Not for a moment.

Laura's Room

is more untidy than ever. Flakes of her skin and hair
cloud surfaces, strands entangle in abandoned brush.
Books totter where favoured ones have been removed.
Bedding rises like a monster with quilted tentacles.
It's not a monument — more a work in progress.
Each visit she takes away one more piece.

Salve

I dreamed I saw someone strike you,
a shocking slap which lacerated
your white neck with a deep welt.

I leapt in anger as your eyes
shocked with tears, though you
are a woman grown.

I wiped the blood with soft cloth,
delicately dabbed arnica as you winced.
It was already staining your skin blue.

How can I reach you now with salve?
So much simpler when you were
close to my arms and healing hands.

A Posy for our Daughter on her Wedding Day

Lavender's blue spires, for you to remember
how you gather it for jellies, scones and scent;
Forget-me-nots as blue as your eyes, like
those of the grandmother you never met.
Briar roses: their pinks harden into hips
as your love ripens and strengthens.
White feverfew to soothe your ills,
pansies, always, for thoughts, our daughter,
as you set out on this marvellous journey,
your beloved beside you. Holding hands,
you step into your future together.
Take this posy, made of love. It will never decay.

Letting Go

First you hold them like a secret
you only suspect is true.
Then soft knockings from within
tap out messages for you.
Slowly the body allows escape,
you hold them in your arms,
dazed and milky, full of love,
pledged to defend from harm.
Then you hold them to your heart
and put them to the breast.
But they learn to walk away
like any other guest.

About this Collection

Author photo courtesy of Angela Topping

These poems have been written over a long period of time, in response to how it felt to be a child, to mature, to become a parent and to see my own children mature.

I was lucky to have parents who talked to me, and developed my love of story and nature. Both died when I was in my twenties, so never met my children. I have continued to talk to them through my poetry.

Being breastfed myself, I was keen to do the same. The National Childbirth Trust provided a network of other breastfeeding mums and my sister gave me confidence with her advice. For a few years I edited the local NCT magazine, *Storktalk*. After a career in education, I now make my living as a freelance writer and poet. I enjoy tutoring, leading workshops and giving readings.

It has been a pleasure to make this selection of my work and I am grateful to Teika Bellamy for inviting me to do so.

*

If you want to know more about me, my blog is:
http://angelatopping.wordpress.com
My website is at http://www.angelatopping.com
and there is further information at:
http://en.wikipedia.org/wiki/Angela_Topping

Mother's Milk Books

is an independent press, founded and managed by at-home mother, Dr Teika Bellamy.

The aim of the press is to publish high-quality, beautiful books that normalize breastfeeding. Mother's Milk Books also produces and sells art and poetry prints, as well as greetings cards. For more information about the press, and to make purchases from the online store, please visit: www.mothersmilkbooks.com